The Homosexual Way— A Christian Option?

by

David Field

Senior Tutor, Oak Hill Theological College, London

GROVE BOOKS

BRAMCOTE NOTTS.

CONTENTS

First Impression January 1976

ISSN 0305 4241

ISBN 0 901710 83 0

1. CLEARING THE GROUND

'We now realise', wrote the compilers of the British Council of Churches' Report on *Sex and Morality,* 'that homosexuality and other abnormalities are far commoner than used to be thought.'[1]

If the conclusion rocked the Christian world in 1966 (and reactions to this particular section of the B.C.C. Report suggest that it did), it provides a rather sad commentary on the ostrich-like capacity of Christian people to shut their eyes to the facts of life around them. It is matched by the unfortunately revealing remark in the Interpreter's Bible, commenting on the reference to homosexuality in Rom. 1.27, that 'the subject is one which in honesty must be faced, but on which no man of fine feeling would care to linger'.

Historians, anthropologists and sociologists agree that the current preoccupation with the rights and wrongs of homosexuality reflects the new freedom with which all matters of sex are discussed, and not a dramatic rise in the number of practising homosexuals over recent years. Anthropological investigations among primitive tribes reveal well-established (though not always approved) patterns of homosexual behaviour. Cross-culturally, too, the pattern seems to be fairly even. In 1957 the Wolfenden Committee concluded that 'homosexuality is not, in spite of the widely held belief to the contrary, peculiar to members of particular professions or social classes; nor, as it is sometimes supposed, is it peculiar to the intelligentsia. Our evidence shows that it exists among all callings and at all levels of society.'[2]

Statistics

How widespread is homosexuality in Britain today? Reliable statistics are notoriously hard to come by, but in medical circles opinion is hardening that the figure may be as high as 5% of the total population. (This, of course, relates to those with homosexual tendencies; even in the more permissive climate prevailing today, the number who actually practise as homosexuals is probably lower). In his much-publicized survey of adult white males in the United States, Dr. Kinsey found that 4% of the men he interviewed confessed to being exclusively homosexual, while a further 6% said they had been more or less exclusively homosexual for at least three years between the ages of 16 and 65. Estimates for Britain tend to be lower, but nonetheless significant. Representative among them are those of Norman Pittenger, who reckons that about 5% of British men and women are either latent or active homosexuals; and of F. E. Kenyon who, in his B.M.A. booklet, quotes a figure of 1 in 25 for men and 1 in 45 for women.

Those who put forward these figures are the first to admit that they do so only tentatively. Nevertheless, the commercial viability of magazines aimed at the homosexual market (many of them undoubtedly as nauseating to most homosexuals as similar literature aimed at their heterosexual counterparts) strongly suggests that such estimates are not grossly inflated. If the proportions are even only approximate, it is worthwhile pausing to translate

[1] *Sex and Morality* (S.C.M.) p.13.
[2] *Report of the Committee on Homosexual Offences and Prostitution* (H.M.S.O.), p.17.

the cold statistics into more familiar terms. In a middle-sized comprehensive school employing a teaching staff of 65, three of the teachers are likely to have homosexual leanings. On the sporting scene, if all the homosexuals were taken out of a crowd watching an international football match and transferred to an average fourth division game, they would just about equal the normal gate. In pastoral terms, a minister preaching to a congregation of 200 should *expect* nine or ten of his people to have a homosexual orientation.

These illustrations may help to put the problem into perspective. The incidence of homosexuality is too widespread to be ignored, especially by Christians who are encouraged by the Bible to show special concern for minority groups.

An important distinction

The modern debate on homosexuality has thrown up some important distinctions; notably the difference between the *pervert* and the *invert.*

In popular discussion, it is often assumed that homosexuality and perversion are synonymous. All people are naturally heterosexual; therefore, all homosexuals are perverts. But to make this kind of assumption is to fly in the face of the facts modern research has made available to us. It is undoubtedly true that many young men and women, heterosexual by nature, are drawn into student Gay Societies and other homosexual circles from a desire to experiment with the unusual, or to find (what is for them) unorthodox stimulation. Some, especially those in mono-sex institutions like boarding schools, prisons and some branches of the armed forces, may drift into homosexual practice as the only available outlet for their sexual drive. There will always be others, too, who are frankly attracted by anything which is either illegal or frowned upon by society—as the homosexual Westermarck knew who, in the old days, 'would be very sorry to see the English law changed, as the practice would then lose its charm.'

To describe this kind of life-style as perverted is not libellous. Nevertheless, if all those who have been drawn away from their natural heterosexual orientation are left out of the reckoning, there still remains a significant number—probably the majority of all homosexuals—who can never remember being attracted to members of the opposite sex. These people are inverts, not perverts. For them, homosexual attraction seems perfectly natural. Many of them struggle to suppress their sexual drive out of fear or respect for a society which frowns on homosexual relationships. Quite a few get married and have children, in a frantic attempt to become and appear 'normal'.

The causes of homosexual inversion have been a matter of debate for a long time. Many case histories support the view that abnormalities in family life are a major causative factor. D. J. West, for example, concluded from a survey he conducted at the Maudsley Hospital that 'it was the combination of unsatisfactory father and mother which was particularly characteristic of the male homosexual patients' backgrounds.'[1] Kinsey, too, leaned towards a socio-psychological explanation for confirmed homosexual tendencies. Others, however, have pointed to the possibility of a biological explanation. For many years, hormonal imbalance was considered to be a root cause of homosexuality. Tests have failed to substantiate this suspicion, but research provides some encouragement for the view that genetic and chromosomal factors may play a significant part in the formation of homosexual life-patterns.

Probably no single explanation can cover all cases. But doubts about causation must not be allowed to obscure the ethical significance of homosexual inversion. Those who have never known any physical attraction for the opposite sex can hardly be blamed for their condition. It seems self-evident that to reproach a practising invert for behaving 'unnaturally' is nonsensical. Is it not therefore right for the Christian moralist to condone the *invert's* homosexual life-style—in the interests of understanding and compassion—while remaining absolutely adamant in condemning the *pervert?* That, as we shall see, is the conclusion many influential churchmen are inviting us to draw.

1 D. J. West, *Homosexuality* (Pelican), p.185.

2. SOCIAL ATTITUDES

From the time of Gibbon's epic on the fall of the Roman Empire, homosexuality has been widely regarded as a sinister threat to the security of society. And, inevitably, this strong social disapproval has found expression in British Law. An Act passed in 1290 laid it down that a convicted sodomite was to be buried alive. Henry VIII changed the mode of execution in 1533, but it was not until 1861 that life imprisonment was substituted for the death penalty.

Strange though it may seem in retrospect, a man convicted of buggery before 1967 could be sentenced to spend the rest of his life in jail. Since then, as a result of the Sexual Offences Act (for which the Wolfenden Report, published ten years previously, had paved the way), criminal charges can no longer be preferred against consenting males over the age of 21, who perform homosexual acts in private.

A curious feature of this recent law—and, indeed, of previous legislation—is that the practice of lesbianism is virtually ignored.

Misconceptions

Two misconceptions about the social effects of homosexuality can be cleared away fairly quickly.

In the first place, it is often maintained that all homosexual men pose a direct threat to the safety of young children.

If this were true, a strong case could be made for outlawing all homosexual behaviour. The evidence, however, falls a long way short of proof. Individual homosexuals are convicted of sexual offences against children; but then so are individual heterosexuals too. Dr. Faith Spicer concluded, after a special survey, that 'a homosexual is no more likely to be a pederast than a heterosexual to want to assault young girls.'[1]

Proportionately to their total numbers (assuming that the one-in-twenty estimate is roughly correct), it seems grossly unjust to accuse homosexuals, *as a group,* of putting youngsters at moral risk, whatever one's personal views about the rights and wrongs of homosexuality in general. Clearly, parents are regularly entrusting their children to homosexual teachers and doctors without being in the least aware that they are doing so. The fact that those in these professions with a homosexual orientation are hard to pick out, argues very strongly against the view that homosexuality, as such, constitutes a special danger to the very young. Where a youngster is sexually assaulted, the most potent factor is likely to be a breakdown in self-control on the part of the assailant—and that is a fault common to both homosexuals and heterosexuals.

Then secondly, it is sometimes assumed that homosexuality constitutes a serious threat to the stability of marriage and family life.

In this respect, a formidable mountain of evidence can be stacked against the homosexual. The Gay Liberation Front, in particular, has as one of its central aims the abolition of family life. Carl Wittman's *Gay Manifesto,* which sparked off the British branch of the G.L.F., attacks Christianity specifically as the creed of a group 'whose archaic and irrational teaching supports the family and marriage as the only permanent condition for sex.'

[1] F. Spicer, *Sex and the Love Relationship* (Priory Press), pp.86f.

It is a pity that the G.L.F. is uncritically accepted by so many as the mouthpiece of homosexual opinion. Many homosexuals (probably the majority) are embarrassed by its methods and regret its more vociferous pronouncements. Even those who seek some kind of relationship through the advertisement columns of papers like *Gay News* often go out of their way to disown the 'gay scene'. Several other less publicized homophile organizations, like *Parents Enquiry,* exist with the stated intention of upholding the standards of marriage and family life which the G.L.F. so strenuously opposes.

The growing popularity of homosexual marriage ceremonies, however one may view the theological and social reasoning behind them, bears its own witness to the desire of many invert couples to stabilize their relationships in a socially acceptable way. Very few homosexuals would go along with the G.L.F. in its attempts to smash marriage as an institution. Many would crave the benefits of a close family life-style for themselves.

Disgust or Outrage?

Ruthless scrutiny of the foundations on which popular opinions about homosexuality are based raises an even more radical and disturbing question. How far is the heterosexual majority's abhorrence of homosexual behaviour a projection of their disgust at a minority's life-style, rather than an expression of legitimate moral outrage?

It is easy to demonstrate that a great deal of revulsion is morally irrelevant. I may be horrified at the thought of a snake in my garden or a wasp in my bathroom, but my hostile feelings do not make all snakes and wasps bad things. The sight of a man swallowing raw bacon-rinds may leave me physically nauseated, but my feelings of revulsion do not necessarily invalidate his conduct ethically. On the other hand, if I find myself a witness when an old lady is mugged, the incident may leave me disgusted *and* convinced that such an act of assault is morally (as well as legally) wrong. Where does homosexuality stand in this scale of comparison? Is it possible to distinguish between moral indignation and distaste?

To sharpen the question still further, it is important to recognize the immensely powerful influence social conditioning has on the forming of our opinions about sexual conduct. Among the people of some cultures, anal intercourse is not viewed with distaste; but the same people may well find the western practice of kissing mouths immensely distasteful. If we find particular customs and practices culturally alien, are we thereby justified in condemning them as immoral? Very strong, opinion-forming pressures can be discerned behind at least some of our inbuilt approaches to conduct between people of the same sex. Two girls, for example, may greet each other in the street with a kiss, and then walk off arm-in-arm—without any social disapproval. But if two British boys express their affection publicly in a similar way, they are greeted with howls of moral outrage (though no-one would mind them kissing cheeks if they were French). Apart from cultural indoctrination, how are we to explain this kind of discrimination?

Norman Pittenger observes that many protests against expressions of affection between members of the same sex 'seem to be nothing more than rationalizations of a sense of disgust or horror at the very thought of such physical acts'.[1] His words are too near the truth to be dismissed lightly. Certainly, as far as physical expressions of *friendship* are concerned, it is all too easy to muddle righteous indignation with inhibition.

The case of the adolescent

There is, however, one argument in the social sector which bears much closer examination. If there is insufficient evidence to convict homosexuals, as a class, of being a danger to the very young, there is a much stronger case to answer as far as adolescents are concerned. Faith Spicer may be perfectly correct in maintaining that there are just as many seductions among heterosexuals as among homosexuals, but the force of her conclusion must not be allowed to obscure an important point of difference. Heterosexuals, generally speaking, corrupt other heterosexuals; but homosexuals, very often, corrupt heterosexuals—especially in the teen-age bracket.

For a long time now, psychologists have been telling us that the average teenager passes through a stage, en route (usually) to a fully heterosexual orientation, when he or she is particularly susceptible to homosexual advances. Many happily married heterosexual young men could testify to a time, shortly after puberty, when some kind of sexual by-play with another boy took precedence over the much more difficult business of forming relationships with girls. For most adults such incidents are just embarrassing memories. For just a few—but still a significant minority—this homosexual experience marks the beginning of a life-long incapacity to form heterosexual relationships. They remain at a stage of sexual development most of their peers pass through.

How many of these young people would have turned out to be invert homosexuals anyway is impossible to say, but a weighty case can clearly be made out for protecting those whose sexual orientation is finely balanced from the dominating influence of older homosexuals, at a time when they are particularly vulnerable to such approaches. In the Polytechnic era, when school-leavers mix freely with mature students, this raises a particularly large question-mark against the current National Union of Students' campaign to encourage the formation of Gay Societies. If it is still right, as it surely is, to protect the very young against those who would exploit them sexually, college authorities cannot be blamed for doing their best to protect adolescent students from those who might hinder their growth into full heterosexuality, by opposing this apparently liberal N.U.S. policy.

This argument is based, however, on a presupposition which many (including the N.U.S.) would flatly reject. It can only be wrong to retard a young person, temporarily or otherwise, from heterosexual development if a homosexual life-style is to be considered second-best. Words like 'exploit' and 'protect' make this assumption. But is it a fair one? Can we be as sure as our grandfathers were that homosexual behaviour is either wrong in itself, or at any rate unsatisfactory as an alternative to a 'normal' heterosexual life-style?

[1] N. Pittenger, *Time for Consent* (S.C.M.), p.107.

3. THE BIBLE'S TEACHING

To discover whether homosexuality is intrinsically right or wrong, the Christian will want to turn first to the biblical evidence. There is not a great deal of it, but what there is seems to load the scales heavily against a permissive view of homosexual behaviour.

The Old Testament

In the Old Testament, there are two extended passages which have traditionally been thought to show homosexuality in a particularly bad light. The first, in Genesis 19, concerns the incident from which the term 'sodomy' takes its origin. In his home in the city of Sodom, Lot was offering hospitality to two messengers of God Abraham had already entertained by the Oaks of Mamre. With intentions Lot immediately recognized as hostile, the men of the city, ('all the people to the last man'—v.4), surrounded the house and demanded the surrender of his two guests. With great courage, Lot went out to parley with them and, when words failed, offered his two virgin daughters instead of the men. When this did not satisfy the mob, we are told that Lot himself would have suffered, but for the timely intervention of his heavenly visitors. The destruction of Sodom follows immediately, and the implication is that the men of Sodom's homosexual intentions were at least partly responsible for the divine judgment their city suffered.

The account of the second incident, in Judges 19, follows a very similar pattern. A traveller, arriving late in the evening at the city of Gibeah with his concubine and servant, is offered hospitality by an elderly resident. Hearing that a stranger was in town, the men of the city ('base fellows'—v.22) demand that the guest be brought out. His host refuses but, like Lot, offers them a substitute sacrifice—his own virgin daughter and his guest's concubine. The offer is not well received, but the concubine is sent out nevertheless, and they 'abused her all night until morning' (v.25), leaving her a lifeless wreck on the doorstep at daybreak. In this case, the divine judgment that followed was mediated through military action. Gibeah, like Sodom, was severely punished for its citizens' sin. And again the implication is that this sin was fundamentally one of intended homosexual assault.

It seems hard to escape the conclusion, from these two passages, that homosexual behaviour (or even the threat of it) incurs God's judgment. But this interpretation has been seriously challenged in two ways.

D. S. Bailey, in his book *Homosexuality and the Christian Tradition,* maintains that God punished the men of Sodom and Gibeah for breaching the rules of hospitality, not for threatening homosexual assault. On each occasion, he points out, the men asked to *know* the strangers. Their intentions were hostile, but not homosexual. So (he concludes) the chief biblical bastion for the case against homosexuality crumples. The two passages in question are not about sex at all; they are about hospitality.

Bailey's arguments have received a surprising measure of support in books which aim to deal with the biblical approach to homosexuality—an enthusiasm which is particularly strange in view of the coolness with which his interpretation has been received by commentators on the text. In both passages this view involves taking the word 'know' in completely different senses in the space of four verses (Gen. 19.5, 8; Jud. 19.22, 25). Much more seriously, it fails to explain why on each occasion the host replied to a request for a formal introduction by offering his daughter for sexual abuse—and why the visitor's concubine was so severely assaulted at Gibeah. It also raises serious doubts about the interpretation the New Testament puts on the punishment of Sodom (in Jude 7). Bailey's explanations outreach many of his readers' credulity. In Derek Kidner's words, 'the doubt created by Dr. Bailey has travelled more widely than the reasons he produces for it. Not one of these reasons, it may be suggested, stands any serious scrutiny.'[1]

There seems no reasonable doubt that the mobs at Sodom and Gibeah were bent on homosexual assault. But this fact, in itself, raises a second and more serious question about the legitimacy of using these two Old Testament incidents to support a blanket condemnation of all homosexuality.

An assault is as different from a gesture of love as chalk is from cheese. Few, if any, members of Gay Lib. would plead that freedom for homosexuals should be extended to make sexual assault permissible. If the Bible's condemnation of homosexuality is directed only against those who would force their favours on unwilling partners, dissenters are likely to be few. The liberty for which the G.L.F. fights is freedom for a homosexual couple to express their feelings with full consent on both sides. Is there any indication that the Bible condemns *that* kind of homosexual liaison?

Apart from the fairly lengthy accounts of the attempted assaults at Sodom and Gibeah, other Old Testament references to homosexuality are confined to isolated verses. In Lev. 18.22 and 20.13, male homosexual practice is labelled as an 'abomination' for which the death penalty is prescribed. The first book of Kings echoes the same theme; the presence of male prostitutes in the land is condemned, and their removal accepted as a sign of spiritual reformation (1 Kings 14.24, 15.12, 22.46). To complete the picture, one might add the condemnation of transvestism in Deut. 22.5.

Again, the case against homosexuality seems cast-iron. But the suggestion has been made that if these scattered but clear-cut Old Testament references are seen in their correct *religious* context, their condemnatory tone is softened. Racially mixed marriages, it is pointed out, are also forbidden by the Old Testament, but the reasons behind the ban are religious, not ethical. The target of the veto is the importing of foreign gods, not the marrying of foreign brides. Male prostitution, too, was an import from pagan worship, as was transvestism. Interpreted against the background of their historical setting, therefore, these verses forbid idolatrous homosexual practices, but appear to say nothing about homosexual behaviour which has no religious overtones.

Can we conclude, then, that the Law's ban on homosexual behaviour is just a codification of God's judgment on idolatry and the kind of sexual

[1] F. D. Kidner, *Genesis* (Tyndale Press), p.137.

assault typified by the incidents at Sodom and Gibeah? Is it fair to argue that the Old Testament has nothing to say against physical love-making between two invert homosexuals who simply want the liberty their heterosexual friends enjoy to express their fondness for one another in a physical way—without any hint of idolatrous worship? It is impossible to answer either question with a simple 'yes'. Although the biblical writers' main target is casual sex with religious overtones, a loving homosexual relationship cannot be excluded from their overall ban. The context of the law against homosexual behaviour in Leviticus includes condemnation of intercourse with blood-relations and adultery, as well as prostitution and bestiality. Either of the former can, as we know, be the consummation of a relationship which is every bit as tender and affectionate as the love-bond between two men or two women. The biblical ban extends to all four sets of circumstances, despite the immense heart-ache involved for all concerned in abstaining from the full physical expression of their feelings.

The New Testament

Clear references to homosexuality in the New Testament are very few indeed.

Jesus himself, as far as we can tell from the four Gospels, never expressed his views on the subject publicly. He seems to have been far more concerned with sins of the mind and heart (like pride, greed and selfishness)—an important corrective, perhaps, to the twentieth century's preoccupation with sex.

Apart from the allusion to the sin of Sodom in Jude, all the New Testament's references to homosexuality come from Paul's pen. Paul is rather more explicit than Jesus because he was dealing with Gentile converts whose moral environment was far more permissive than that of the Jews to whom Jesus spoke. But, as might be expected from a man steeped in the Old Testament Scriptures, his tone is condemnatory.

In *Romans 1,* he describes one result, in the sexual sphere, of a life given over to the things of creation rather than to God the Creator: 'Their women exchanged natural relations for unnatural, and the men likewise gave up natural relations with women and were consumed with passion for one another, men committing shameless acts with men and receiving in their own persons the due penalty for their error' (vv.25f.). It is interesting to notice, in passing, that Paul is more realistic about lesbianism than the British law, which has virtually ignored it.

In *1 Cor. 6.9* he is more brief but equally explicit; among the 'unrighteous' who will not inherit the Kingdom of God are 'homosexuals' (the RSV uses the one English word to translate the two Greek words Paul himself used to indicate the roles of the two partners in a homosexual union). Then finally, in *1 Tim. 1.10,* 'sodomites' are listed among the 'lawless and disobedient' who stand under the condemnation of God's law.

Conclusive though these few references may seem in their censure of homosexual behaviour, attempts have been made to show that Paul only had one minority group of homosexuals in mind when he wrote—the perverts. The New English Bible appears to favour this restricted interpretation in its translation of all three of the relevant passages from the

Epistles. In Romans, the men who 'behave indecently with males' are 'paid in their own persons the fitting wage of such *perversion*'. In 1 Corinthians, the neutral 'homosexuals' of the RSV comes across as 'homosexual *perversion*'. And in 1 Timothy *'perverts'* (instead of 'sodomites') appear alongside the murderers, the fornicators and the others whom God's law condemns.

These translations invite the conclusion they suggest. Paul's strong words, it is implied, were directed only against those who dabbled in homosexuality out of sheer curiosity or supersensuality. Such perversion incurs God's wrath—and justly so, because this kind of homosexual conduct on the part of *hetero*sexuals drags the whole of homosexuality into disrepute. But on the subject of inversion, Paul is silent. Apparently the New Testament has nothing to say in condemnation of the man or woman whose sexual orientation drives him or her into an intimate, lasting relationship with a member of the same sex.

Contextual evidence is brought in to support the case. Paul is addressing his remarks on homosexuality in Romans to men who (he says) have 'given up natural relations with women'. But *invert homosexuals have no such relations to give up.* Paul's stern words cannot, therefore, be construed as a blanket condemnation of all homosexuality. So too in 1 Corinthians, after the slighting reference to homosexuals in verse 9, he goes on to deplore heterosexual relations with a prostitute. If his main target in this chapter is the ephemeral abuse of sex typified by the 'one-night stand', his words cannot, again, be taken to apply to the average invert, who longs for a stable, loving relationship just as much as the average heterosexual. Similarly, the context of 1 Timothy 1.10 embraces those who set out to wreck all precious human relationships, by killing and lying as well as by indulging in sexual deceit; so once more, the invert whose heartfelt aim it is to cement rather than to smash relationships cannot be included under this particular condemnation.

This argument from context is clearly crucial. If, in the light of modern knowledge, Paul's words can be understood to absolve the invert from censure, the traditionally hostile approach of biblical theology to all homosexuality is overdue for reappraisal. We must therefore examine the theological context of Paul's teaching much more closely to discover how far his ban can be taken to extend today. In the meantime, however, it is only fair to point out that the linguistic prop the New English Bible lends to this view is inadequate to take the strain.

If the NEB's aim is to reflect the modern distinction between perversion and inversion, its translation of the relevant verses rests on very shaky foundations indeed. The Greek words Paul used do not make this distinction at all. The most common word *(arsenokoites)* covers both invert and pervert, and when Paul does make any kind of distinction between homosexuals (in 1 Cor. 6.9) it is to include, specifically, both partners in a homosexual union under the umbrella of the same condemnation, and not to exclude the invert majority from the censure he is weighing out to the pervert fringe.

4. THE THEOLOGICAL PERSPECTIVE

Three major areas of biblical doctrine impinge upon any discussion of homosexuality from a Christian angle. The doctrine of *sex* is obviously highly relevant; the doctrine of *creation* is crucial to the debate about homosexual inversion; and above them both towers the doctrine of *love,* under which Christ subsumed all the ethical teaching of the Old Testament.

The Doctrine of Sex

The traditional Christian view of sex is still occasionally pilloried as a kill-joy approach which concentrates attention on the making of babies, while drawing a modest veil over the extreme pleasure the process of conception involves. The suggestion in some quarters is that God added the pleasure as an inducement to intercourse, to ensure the continuation of the race; but to focus on the pleasure, without the intention to procreate, is to do something faintly distasteful and sub-Christian. 'It is not always appreciated', writes Anthony Storr, 'that, even today, the orthodox Christian attitude towards sex is, when one considers the generality of mankind, exceptionally severe; . . . the idea that sexual abstinence is an expression of a superior morality, and that celibacy is to be equated with virtue is still widely held, especially by those who belong to churches which insist that their clergy shall not marry.'[1]

At its most crude, this is a grotesque misrepresentation of the biblical approach to sex. The Scriptures vibrate with delight in the physical intimacies a man and his wife enjoy. 'Rejoice in the wife of your youth', advises the ever-practical book of Proverbs. 'Let her affection fill you at all times with delight, be infatuated always with her love.'[2] And Paul, who was no woman-hater, publicly dissociates himself from 'liars whose consciences are seared, who forbid marriage . . . For everything created by God is good, and nothing is to be rejected if it is received with thanksgiving.'[3] It comes as no surprise to find that the early canonists relegated the *Acts of John,* a pseudo-Christian document which describes sexual intercourse as 'an experiment of the serpent', to the deeper shadows of the Apocrypha.

Nevertheless, it has to be admitted that in the history of the church there have always been teachers of influence who have played down the role of physical love-making. The medieval church, in particular, was obsessed with its self-imposed duty of limiting the expression of sexual intimacy. The old confessors' manuals, with their detailed descriptions of the positions in which a married couple could or could not rightly enjoy sexual intercourse, make strange and rather sad reading today. Very few Christians indeed would look to this kind of literature for authoritative guidance now, but the scar of the past is still sometimes faintly visible. We can be sincerely grateful for the more liberal attitude to the enjoyment of sex which prevails in our time, if only because it marks a return to the very positive teaching of the Bible.

1 A. Storr, *Sexual Deviation* (Pelican), p.19.
2 Prov. 5.18f.
3 1 Tim. 4.2ff.

With the renewed, biblical emphasis on the importance of sex in establishing and deepening the love a married couple should have for one another, questions about the rights and wrongs of particular expressions of physical intimacy demand brave answers. Some such expressions of affection, deeply private though they may be to the couple concerned, are so common-place that no eyebrows would be raised if the details were made public. Others still tend to shock us. But why? If any sexual act, done with the mutual consent of both partners, increases the love and respect the one has for the other, on what grounds can it be declared wrong? The theological and ethical rationale for denying such intimacies as fellatio—or even anal intercourse—to a married couple seems very tenuous indeed.

The implications for homosexual behaviour are important. None of the things that a homosexual couple do together is peculiar to those with a homosexual orientation. Every one of these intimacies may be—and is, if the findings of questionnaires are to be trusted—practised by some married heterosexual couples too. Even anal intercourse is probably a more common practice (proportionately) among heterosexuals than among the homosexual members of society. The majority of married couples would doubtless find this a distasteful way of expressing their love, but by no means all of them. The ethical grounds for condemning homosexuals *simply for what they do* are therefore very flimsy.

Many, however, would find much safer ground in condemning homosexual behaviour, theologically and ethically, for the wedge it drives between the *relational* and *procreational* purposes of sexual intercourse. However much we may applaud the re-establishment of the importance of sex in cementing relationships, Christian doctrine will not allow us to divorce the relational aspect of sex from the procreational, which is an equally important dimension in God's overall plan. Homosexual couples, inevitably, make this division. Therefore (many Christians would conclude) what they do together must be labelled as wrong.

Looking back to the teaching of Thomas Aquinas, Roman Catholicism is particularly adamant in treating the link between the relational and procreational purposes of sexual intercourse as theologically indissoluble. The conclusion, as far as homosexuality is concerned, is clear and unmistakable. In Aquinas' own words, 'every homosexual act between males is against nature and inconsistent with right reason, since it necessarily involves the pursuit of venereal pleasure in such a way as to exclude the possibility of generation.'

Many influential Protestant scholars have taken a rather different line. While respecting the importance of having children, and insisting that the only right context for sexual intercourse is marriage, they do not regard the relational and procreational aspects of sex as two things God has indivisibly linked. As far as marriage is concerned, this view leads logically (and against the Roman Catholic position) to an endorsement of the use of contraceptives. The implications for homosexuality are rarely spelled out so fully. But if it is allowable, from a Christian point of view, to use sex for the establishing and deepening of a relationship without (necessarily) carrying with it the possibility of starting a baby, it seems difficult to fault homosexuals for expressing their affection physically, just because procreation is in their case impossible.

Scripturally, support for both views may be drawn from the first two chapters of Genesis. Catholics, taking both creation accounts together, would conclude that God's procreational (1.27f.) and relational (2.24) purposes for sex are indivisible. Protestants, on the other hand, would point out that in neither account are the two purposes specifically linked; and it is Gen. 2.24 (with its stress on relationship) that is used as a blueprint for marriage in the New Testament.

It would be wrong to polarize the differences too sharply. The debate continues, and powerful mediating influences are not lacking.[1] Suffice it to say for our purposes that *if* the Protestant position is tenable, we have yet to find a convincing doctrinal reason for condemning homosexuals *simply for what they do.*

The Doctrine of Creation

It is at this point that the apparently slender body of New Testament teaching on homosexuality calls for re-examination. As well as its *historical* setting, every piece of biblical teaching has a *theological* context too.

As we have seen, when viewed against their historical background, Paul's condemnations of homosexual behaviour appear (in the light of modern distinctions) to be directed against the pervert rather than the invert; and the horrors of doing ethics by proof-text underline the importance of reading the Epistles in their historical context. But it is equally important, if we are to do justice to the full force of what Paul is saying, to discover the theological setting into which he deliberately builds his ethical teaching on homosexuality.

In Romans 1, the theological context is *creation.* After setting up the headlines of his theme in vv.16-18 (the glory of the gospel, in contrast to human sin which attracts God's judgment), Paul expands on the horrors of man's predicament. His aim is to show how, both spiritually and morally, mankind has made a bad exchange. Man was created to honour God, but 'exchanged the glory of the immortal God' for futile God-substitutes (vv.19-23). This bad spiritual exchange led to moral breakdown too (vv.26, 27); and in spelling out just one consequence of this distortion of values, Paul resorts to exchange language once more—'their women exchanged natural relations for unnatural, and the men likewise . . .'

This creation context throws a completely new light on the meaning of the words 'natural relations' in verses 26 and 27. As we have seen, some would fasten on this expression to provide an escape-clause for the invert

1 e.g. P. Ramsey, *One Flesh* (Grove Booklet on Ethics no. 8).

homosexual. For the *in*vert, relations with a member of the opposite sex are *un*natural; he (or she) has never made this exchange of natural for unnatural which Paul condemns. It may be right to call such a person 'abnormal' (in the sense of belonging to a minority group in a predominantly heterosexual society), but surely 'unnatural" is the wrong word to use?

It is the theological context of Paul's words that make this interpretation untenable. In writing about 'natural relations', Paul is not referring to individual men and women *as they are.* His canvas is much broader. He is taking the argument back ,far more radically, to man and woman *as God created them.* By 'unnatural' he means 'unnatural to mankind in God's creation pattern'. And that pattern he clearly understands to be heterosexual. So the distinction between pervert and invert (which Paul could hardly have made anyway) is undercut. The 'exchange' he has in mind is not just the capricious sex-swapping of the pervert in his search for fresh stimulation, but the divergence *all* homosexual behaviour represents from God's creation scheme. When set in the context of creation, all homosexual relations are 'unnatural relations'.

On the basis of Paul's words in Romans, then, the Christian has to take issue with Kinsey when he claims that 'homosexuality has been a significant part of human sexual activity ever since the dawn of history, primarily because it is an expression of capacities which are basic in the human animal.' An invert may feel that for him or her homosexual behaviour is perfectly natural. But that does not alter the theological fact that for mankind as a whole homosexuality is as unnatural as idolatry. Somewhere along the line, a 'bad exchange' has taken place.

Once the creation context of Romans 1 is identified, the theological settings of the other two references to homosexuality in the New Testament become extremely interesting and significant.

In 1 Timothy 1, the context is an updated version of the Ten Commandments. Paul is defining the place of moral law—and in particular of the Decalogue—in the Christian life. He does not quote the commandments explicitly, but the Old Testament wording is only just below the surface. First come four words that list offences against God, covering, in brief the first four Commandments (the 'ungodly and sinners' in verse 9 are those who have no reverence for God but actively oppose him; and the 'unholy and profane' are those who regard nothing as sacred, whether the Lord's Name or his Day). Next come references to 'murderers of fathers and mothers' (the opposite of 'honouring' them—the fifth commandment), and 'manslayers' (contrast 'thou shalt not kill'). The word 'kidnappers' (v.10) provides an interesting parallel to the eighth commandment, 'thou shalt not steal' (there was a thriving black market in kidnapped slaves at Ephesus); while 'liars and perjurers' mirror the ninth commandment rather more obviously. The final words in the list ('whatever else . . .') seem an oddly cavalier way to dismiss the tenth commandment on covetousness, but they probably reflect Paul's lack of concern at this point for sins of the mind and heart.

It is in the middle of this intriguing list that we find the reference to 'immoral persons' and 'sodomites'. Both words refer to those who engage in sexual intercourse outside marriage, heterosexual or homosexual; and as an interpretation of the seventh commandment the parallel is striking. The implication is that homosexual conduct infringes the demands of the Decalogue as certainly as heterosexual adultery.

Even more significant, however, especially in the light of Romans 1, is the inclusion of homosexuality in an exposition of the Ten Commandments. Scholars have shown that the Decalogue has its theological and ethical roots deep in the creation teaching of Genesis.[1] In other words, the Decalogue's appeal is for men and women to live the life-style the Creator intended for his creation. And in that creation scheme, as Paul has already shown in his letter to the Romans, homosexuality has no place. It may well be that the apostle had the promiscuous pervert at Ephesus in the front of his mind when he wrote 1 Timothy. But the theological context in which he sets this part of his teaching extends to cover all humanity and all homosexuality.

In 1 Cor. 6.9, the same words for 'immoral persons' and 'sodomites' reappear (reinforced by a second word for homosexuals and an explicit reference to adulterers). The theological context, however, is different. Paul is writing to the Corinthians about those who will be excluded from the Kingdom of God. Undoubtedly his primary reference is to casual sex, in which Corinth specialized. But the 'Kingdom' framework in which he sets his words gives them a much wider application. God's Kingdom is not a realm, but a state of affairs in which his rule is acknowledged; his Kingdom comes when his will is done. In other words, a straight line can be drawn, theologically speaking, from God's creation plan (when his will *was* done) through to his Kingdom (when it *is* and *will be* done). And (says Paul) there is no room for homosexual behaviour in the Kingdom. So once more we are faced, not just by a piece of ad hoc advice volunteered to a long-forgotten Christian community with special problems, but by a far-ranging span of teaching on human sexuality which reaches right back to God's creation of man and woman.

Viewed in its theological context, then, the New Testament's teaching on homosexuality takes on an impressive unity. In God's plan, from creation to the coming of his Kingdom, homosexuality has no place. It is only to be expected that God's basic instructions for living, enshrined in the Ten Commandments (which reflect his creation pattern and anticipate his Kingdom), rule out homosexual behaviour altogether. So, despite the very important modern distinction dividing inverts from perverts, it seems impossible to resist the conclusion that the New Testament puts a theological veto on all homosexual behaviour—however well motivated it may be.

[1] cf. C. F. H. Henry, *Christian Personal Ethics,* (Eerdmans), pp.272ff.

But with the mention of motive, some would enter a strong objection at this point. What above *love?* According to an influential line of Christian ethical thinking, popularized in our own day by the exponents of situation ethics, Jesus replaced the Decalogue—and indeed all law-based morality—with an ethic of love. Did he not teach that a loving motive can justify anything?

The Doctrine of Love

The New Testament's teaching on love has been used quite widely to undercut the conclusions of the last section. The question God asks about any homosexual act, it is claimed, is not 'Does it infringe a commandment?', but 'Was it done in love?'. Norman Pittenger, for example, states very bluntly: 'Homosexual acts between persons who intend a permanent union in love are not sinful nor should the church consider them as such.'[1] And Leonard Barnett echoes his liberal sentiments: 'Is it not flagrantly unchristian, unloving', he asks, 'ruthlessly to deny the gay person the right to exercise, responsibly and lovingly, his capacity for love—including sexual loving?'[2]

An interpretation of Christian ethics which stresses love has plenty to commend it. Jesus himself clearly laid enormous emphasis at exactly this point in his moral teaching. He had little time for the unloving paragon of virtue who lives by the rule-book and earns Mark Twain's icy commendation, 'a good man in the worst sense of the word'.

The force of some ancillary arguments brought in to support the situationist's permissive outlook on homosexuality must be admitted too. If we define Christian love in terms of self-giving, it is undoubtedly true that some homosexual relationships are more loving than some heterosexual marriages. As the personal advertisements in *Gay News* testify, many homosexuals desire a strong, loving relationship far more than they do mere genital activity—something which is not always so apparent in similar advertisements placed in periodicals aimed at the 'straight' scene. If we are forced to admit that some acts of sexual intercourse within marriage are immoral when measured by the yardstick of love, are we not at liberty (ask Pittenger and company) to applaud those acts of intimacy between homosexuals which are shown to be truly moral when judged by the same standard? Leonard Barnett certainly thinks so. 'The same Christian rules of sexual morality', he concludes, 'should govern heterosexual behaviour and homosexual behaviour.'[3]

This position is open to all the criticisms levelled at situation ethics. Despite the stress Jesus laid on the necessity of a loving motive, he nowhere taught that a motive of love can justify anything. He never gave his disciples reason to believe that, because of his love-teaching, they could turn a blind eye to the Old Testament laws which labelled some things as bad in themselves, whatever the motive.[4] He was certainly explicit in

1 N. Pittenger, *op. cit.,* p.100.
2 L. Barnett, *Homosexuality* (Gollancz), p.92.
3 *ibid.* p.94.
4 cf. Mt. 5.17ff.

emphasising the importance of the inward thoughts and feelings of a man's sex-life, but there is no hint that he meant his condemnations of extra-marital *hetero*sexual intercourse to apply in cases of bad or mixed motives only. As Michael Ramsey shrewdly observes, 'It is on a deductive theory from the concept of love, and not upon a full examination of Christ's teaching, that the conclusion is being drawn that "nothing of itself can be labelled as wrong".'[1] In other words, in summarizing the Old Testament moral law in his two great love commandments, Jesus was using the word 'love' as a headline, not as an editorial blue pencil.

Replacing all other absolute standards by the single command to love is not only unfaithful to New Testament teaching. It is also patently inadequate as an unsupported prop for moral living. Self-deception and external influences blur love's vision in the best of us. The situationist is the first to admit that those who refuse all directives except that of a loving motive must expect to make many mistakes of moral judgment. Joseph Fletcher looks forward hopefully to the day when some of the errors can be eliminated with the aid of a computer which will help people to make their love calculations more accurately.[2] But the Bible's solution to the problem of mixed motives does not lie in some futuristic ethical Ernie, but in the revealed moral law of God as it is crystallized in the Decalogue and applied by the Holy Spirit. The Decalogue, as we have seen, reflects God's creation plan and anticipates his Kingdom where his will is done perfectly. And on all three counts, homosexual conduct is declared by the New Testament to be wrong. A loving motive—vastly important though it is—cannot reverse that judgment.

[1] A. M. Ramsey, *Image Old and New* (SPCK), p.14.
[2] J. Fletcher, *Situation Ethics* (SCM), pp.177f.

5. ATTITUDES AND ACTION

Must all homosexual behaviour be labelled 'bad'? That is the conclusion to which the biblical evidence clearly points—even in cases where the relationship concerned is deeply affectionate and intended by both parties to be permanent. But does it follow that all practising homosexuals are to blame for what they do?

Blame—and change

It is a fundamental axiom of Christian ethics that a man is only to be blamed for something he can prevent himself from doing. The kleptomaniac's act of theft is always bad, but he is no more to be blamed when he steals than a child with measles is blameworthy because he has spots.

Some writers come close to arguing that, especially for the invert, the homosexual urge may be irresistible. Anthony Storr, for example, writes of 'unhappy, lonely men *driven by a compulsive need* to make contact with others which they may deplore but which they *cannot wholly control*' (the italics are mine).[1] This approach, of course, tends to bracket homosexuality with physical or psychological disease, which is totally unacceptable to a great many homosexuals. But it does substitute healing for punishment as the proper response to those trapped in a behaviour-pattern over which they have no control.

Even so, the sting of blame is not entirely withdrawn. Apart from the 'corporate solidarity' theme which threads its way impressively through the Bible (insisting that the individual must share the responsibility for the pressures his heredity and environment exert upon him), anyone with a disability has a moral duty to submit to a cure. The individual trapped by forces beyond his control still has the responsibility to search for a way out, rather than acquiesce in his condition.

Is there any way of escape for the homosexual who feels that his drive for sexual contact cannot be controlled? Drugs can bring relief from compulsive urges, but in no sense can they be said to effect a cure, and in some cases they produce distressing side-effects. Psychiatry provides various alternatives, ranging from hypnotic suggestion to aversion therapy, but case-studies show an uneven success rate and indicate frequent relapses on the part of some who appear at first to have been helped most by such methods.

Without in the least wishing to polarize medicine and divine power as irreconcilable alternatives (which of course they are not), it is the Christian gospel that offers homosexuals their most radical resource for control. The Bible's claim that the Spirit of Christ can change established behaviour-patterns is too well-attested to be dismissed. Those who enter God's Kingdom by personal commitment to Jesus Christ in faith do not merely place themselves under his rule; they receive his power. The Kingdom demands a change of life-style from every practising homosexual (or rather an *ex*change to God's intended life-style, to use Paul's language). But

1 A. Storr, *op. cit.*, p.90.

along with the demand goes a promise of strength. As the statement on *The Problem of Homosexuality* produced by the Church Information Office guardedly puts it, 'it is a matter of Christian experience that faithful acceptance of a difficult way of life in response to a moral demand always finds reinforcement in a powerful movement from God towards man.'

This position has been challenged by some (churchmen as well as others) as naive, harsh and supercilious. Is the demand for total abstinence—fortified as it may be by the promise of God's strength to overcome temptation—really Christ's good news for homosexuals? 'The attitude which demands of the homosexual no physical expression of his love', claims Norman Pittenger, 'seems to me inhuman, unjust, and above all unchristian.'[1] And Ian Harvey weighs in with a stinging attack on the 'holier-than-thou' attitude which (he feels) typifies many Christians in their negative attitude to homosexuality. 'Since I have seen some of them at work', he writes, 'I have reached the conclusion that had I been in the Colosseum at the time I could well have been on the side of the lions'.[2]

Some of the mud sticks. The condescending approach of the heterosexual Christian who implies by his censorious attitude that homosexuality is out on its own at the top of the sin-league is blatantly out of line with Jesus' ethical emphasis. Jesus repeatedly criticized socially acceptable qualities like aggression and pride, but he said nothing at all (as far as we know) about homosexuality. It is also painfully true that although God works miracles and gives power to conquer habits, he does not always choose to change the orientation of a Christian homosexual. Some, like Alex Davidson, have to fight temptations that persist as long as their sexual drive is strong. The battles are often desperately hard. But (as Davidson himself testifies) the homosexual who is not relieved of his *condition* will always find the Holy Spirit's aid adequate to control his *conduct*.[3] And that, of course, goes for the heterosexual with his different spectrum of temptations too.

The Bible's prescription is self-control through the control of the Spirit. Inevitably, this leads the Christian into sharp conflict with those who would bracket self-control with psychologically harmful repression. Brian Magee, for example, suggests very plausibly that 'the feeling that there is something shameful, something dirty, something sinful about what one *is* is destructive of full development of personality, and of genuine relaxation, or happiness, or spontaneity and freedom . . .'[4] The Christian's reply is that to acknowledge that one is shameful, dirty and sinful is the very first step towards the genuine freedom and happiness which the gospel offers. The Spirit's control is not a harsh demand, but a generously liberating gift. It must follow that those who turn their backs on such a gift cannot be absolved from blame for staying behind the locked door, when they have been offered the key to get out.

1 N. Pittenger, *op. cit.*, p.70.
2 I. Harvey, *To Fall Like Lucifer* (Sidgwick and Jackson).
3 A. Davidson, *Returns of Love* (IVP).
4 B. Magee, *One in Twenty* (Secker and Warburg).

Loneliness—and acceptance

Yet once beyond the door, the outside world can seem a very cold and grey place for a Christian homosexual. However convinced he (or she) may be that the Holy Spirit will more than fill the empty spaces left by old habits and relationships, human loneliness can be something particularly hard to bear. At the dawn of creation God said 'It is not good that man should be alone'; and Eve was created to relieve Adam's loneliness. But how can a modern Adam's loneliness be relieved if no Eve satisfies him, and if he is denied the intimate relationship with another Adam that his heart craves?

In the most poignant terms, many homosexuals define loneliness as their worst enemy. 'You come home to yourself again', confides Alex Davidson, 'and brother, it's so lonely . . . Naturally the answer is that I need a wife . . . someone who will truly be my "other half" . . . the answer is marriage. Which is out of the question.'[1] W. L. Tonge comments soberly, with the vast wealth of the Samaritans' experience behind him, 'The greatest hazard of the homosexual, and the one that leads to suicide, is their spiritual loneliness.'[2]

One might think that the place, above all, where a homosexual could find relief from spiritual loneliness would be the church. Some undoubtedly do discover genuine friendship in a warm church fellowship—but it is probably at the cost of concealing their homosexuality. It may be sobering for church leaders who read this booklet to ask themselves how many of their own people are known to be homosexuals. If the answer is none—or very few—the reason may not be that none (or no more) exist. Even non-practising homosexuals seldom feel secure enough to own up to their 'unnatural' feelings within a Christian fellowship. They fear that if they do, they may be plunged straight back into the lonely blackness they are trying desperately to escape. Significantly, 'Alex Davidson' is only a pen-name—presumably because the author of *Returns of Love* is afraid of discrimination and ostracism, inside as well as outside his Christian group, should his identity be widely publicized.

With the welcome re-emphasis on social responsibility in the church, one might have expected strong words of condemnation from leading churchmen for the social injustice and ostracism many homosexuals suffer. But, with one or two brave exceptions, these have not been forthcoming so far. It is left to Gay Lib. and the N.U.S. to expose the hypocrisy of social bias; and to secular organisations like the National Council for Civil Liberties to fight the strange anomalies of British law, and its even stronger applications in the courts. Even in the educational field, the most obvious sources of help a young invert can find in understanding himself and his feelings are to be found in societies like the Albany Trust, Parents Enquiry and the Campaign for Homosexual Equality—none of which is an avowedly Christian organization. By and large, church spokesmen have maintained an embarrassed silence on the subject; hoping, perhaps, that a problem which affects up to 5% of the men in their congregations may go away of its own accord.

[1] A. Davidson, *op. cit.*, pp.16f.
[2] C. Varah (ed.), *The Samaritans in the 70s* (Constable), pp.176f.

The watchword for all homophile organizations is *acceptance.* It is one the Christian can welcome too—though not wholly without reservation. It implies realism in facing the facts of homosexual life; a welcome for those whom society ostracizes; and a desire to educate both young inverts themselves and those among the heterosexual majority whose attitude towards homosexuals is compounded of suspicion and misunderstanding. It need not, however, imply uncritical recognition of homosexual behaviour as an acceptable alternative life-style.

Realism and education belong together. It is pointless to advise a young homosexual, 'you will grow out of it in the end'. Most young people who feel a homosexual urge do in fact find that it is only a passing stage, but for a significant minority the condition turns out to be permanent. To insist that this need never be so is unrealistic. To allow any young invert to grow up without counsel is educationally unworthy of a society obsessed with the value of education. And to leave up to one person in twenty with no other realistic option than self-concealment is particularly unworthy of a church whose Lord and Master was ready to leave the ninety-nine for the sake of the one.

Heterosexuals need educating too. Both the facts of homosexual inversion and the dangers of type-casting gender roles need appreciating and distinguishing. The advertizers, with their identikit fold-outs of true masculinity and femininity, are responsible for a great deal of confusion here. Measuring his temperament and outlook against the media's image of how a real male ought to feel and react, it is all too easy for a man to think he must be at least half-way to inversion if his responses are not 'normal'. A woman may feel much the same if she is not feminine in quite the way the commercials suggest she ought to be. The 'subtle, shifting blend of masculinity and femininity in one person' to which the National Council of Social Service's report on *Counselling Homosexuals* alludes[1] is a fact of life which would bring enormous relief to many troubled people if only it were better understood and more widely appreciated.

Realism will also dictate frankness in evaluating the way society at large deals with homosexuals. The law of the land is still full of inconsistencies—especially in the way it discriminates between male homosexuality and lesbianism. The punishments meted out to homosexuals in the courts call for critical scrutiny too. When fines on homosexual conduct exceed those imposed for driving offences, serious questions call for urgent answers. Is this a case of a minority (probably unrepresented on the bench) being victimized, while the misdemeanours of a car-owning majority, which may be more socially acceptable but are arguably more dangerous, attract less than realistic penalties? If so, whatever their views on homosexuality, Christians should be among the first to speak out.

The Sexual Law Reform Society also points to the strange fact that under the present law a young man of 16 may get married, but not engage in homosexual conduct until he is over 21. There is good sense in this particular 'anomaly', however. If, as has been shown, homosexuality is only a passing phase for most adolescents, it would be wrong for the law to encourage young people to form lasting homosexual relationships at a stage of sexual development the majority of them will outgrow.

[1] P. Righton (ed.) *Counselling Homosexuals* (Bedford Square Press), p.9.

Many homophile societies whose primary function is educational, also serve as resource-points for friendship. One of the largest, the Campaign for Homosexual Equality, provides social facilities as well as educational material. Another, REACH, sets itself the specific task of providing a focal point of fellowship for isolated homosexuals in the churches, including clergy. As an antidote to loneliness, the efforts of these organizations render a valuable service. Whatever one's attitude to homosexuality, the kind of social ostracism which drives people into a corner where 'sex may be the only source of pleasure to which a man can turn and the only certain way of making any emotional contact with another human being' (Anthony Storr's words[1]) can only be deplored, and efforts to eradicate it applauded.

Nevertheless, for the Christian, there are unsatisfactory features in the approach of these organizations to homosexuality. Although they may, like REACH, welcome 'straight' sympathizers, they tend to be rallying points where homosexuals meet other homosexuals, not places where homosexuals and heterosexuals can share understanding and supportive friendship. And the most disquieting feature of all for those who are convinced from the Bible that practising homosexuals are doing something that God forbids, is that all of them stretch the definition of 'acceptance' to include the admission of stable homosexual unions as an acceptable alternative life-style—whether this is expressed through the encouragement of informal liaisons or in the more elaborate ceremonial of a homosexual 'marriage'.

If homosexual conduct is an aberration from God's creation plan, and finds no place in the life-style of God's Kingdom, it cannot possibly be construed as being within God's will. Abstinence is the only right course for an invert, on Christian grounds.

This plea for self-control may sound harsh. It *is* harsh, if friendship and fellowship are withdrawn along with the possibility of full sexual expression. But it is an important part of the Christian faith that the only proper context for sexual intimacy is heterosexual marriage. Moreover, it is no part of the Christian message that marriage (or its homosexual counterpart) is necessary for genuine personal fulfilment. Jesus Christ himself was a perfectly fulfilled human being, yet he never had sexual intercourse. He was not starved of love through remaining unmarried; on the contrary, he expressed true love perfectly.

The unmarried Christian heterosexual is commanded by the New Testament to avoid sexual liaisons, and the homosexual is under similar discipline. But with Christ's heterosexual example and teaching in mind, one cannot conclude with Dennis Nadin of REACH that 'it is both unrealistic and unloving to deny the homosexual sexual fulfilment'. The path of self-control, hard though it is (for the unmarried heterosexual as well as for the invert), leads to freedom and not to psychological breakdown. But the church must learn to show to its homosexual minority—and to all homosexuals—the depth of understanding, support and open love which Christ requires and which will make a difficult path easier to tread.

1 A. Storr, *op. cit.*, p.90.